INTRODUCTION

OPPOSITE: THE THUKELA FALLS PLUNGE 600 METRES IN FIVE GIANT LEAPS FROM THE TOP OF THE DRAKENSBERG'S AMPHITHEATRE. **ABOVE:** *CLEMATIS BRACHIATA* IS ONE OF THE MYRIAD INDIGENOUS WILD FLOWERS IN THE DRAKENSBERG.

FIRING THE IMAGINATION OF GENERATIONS OF EXPLORERS AND PROVIDING SUPREME CHALLENGES OF MAN AGAINST MOUNTAIN, THE DRAKENSBERG HAS FOR CENTURIES BEEN A MAGNETIC ATTRACTION TO NATURE-LOVERS AND ADVENTURERS. Hikers, bird-watchers and trout fishermen are among the thousands who annually head for the majesty and tranquillity of the mountain range which towers more than 3,000 metres above a natural playground of rolling hills, rivers and pools. Sharp-eyed eagles and vultures are a common sight as they soar below clouds overlooking sandstone overhangs and caves concealing timeless paintings by skilled San (Bushman) hunter-gatherers.

BARRIER OF SPEARS

Originally called uKhahlamba, or the 'barrier of spears' by the Zulu, these formidable mountains were renamed the Drakensberg, or Dragon Mountain, by Boers who thought they resembled a dragon's back. The lower slopes are the Clarens sandstone series, which include fossils of creatures that roamed the planet more than 200 million years ago, while the plateau consists of remnants of a massive outpouring of basalt which once formed a rock-layer more than a kilometre thick.

This range extends for some 1,000 kilometres along South Africa's eastern Escarpment, from Mpumalanga to the Eastern Cape. The highest peaks are in the Maluti-Drakensberg, a 300-kilometre stretch between KwaZulu-Natal and Lesotho. Covering 5,000 square kilometres, the range peaks at 3,482 metres at Lesotho's Thaba Ntlenyana, the highest mountain south of Kilimanjaro. The uKhahlamba-Drakensberg Park, managed by KwaZulu-Natal Wildlife, was recently included in the World Heritage list because of its natural and cultural wealth. The northern region includes the towering Amphitheatre and the Royal Natal National Park; the central section the Giant's Castle Game Reserve; and the south the remote Kamberg and Loteni areas. A management plan is in place to create a transfrontier park that will include the KwaZulu-Natal Wildlife areas, Lesotho's highlands and Sehlabathebe National Park.

OPPOSITE, TOP: HIKING IN GIANT'S CASTLE IN THE CENTRAL BERG. **OPPOSITE, BOTTOM:** THE LOOMING CLIFFS OF THE AMPHITHEATRE. **ABOVE LEFT:** A POCKET OF INDIGENOUS FOREST IN THE ROYAL NATAL NATIONAL PARK. **ABOVE RIGHT:** BASOTHO BOYS PLAYING SOCCER NEAR LESOTHO'S SEHLABATHEBE NATIONAL PARK. **RIGHT:** THE ISOLATED MLAMBONJA VALLEY NEAR CATHEDRAL PEAK IN THE CENTRAL BERG.

ABOVE: A SUMMER VIEW TOWARDS CHAMPAGNE CASTLE IN THE CENTRAL BERG. **BELOW LEFT:** IN SPRINGTIME WILD FLOWERS ATTRACT SCORES OF VIVID SUNBIRDS TO THE LOWER SLOPES. **BELOW RIGHT:** THE GRASSES, WHICH TURN A RICH GREEN IN SUMMER, BIND SOILS ON THE LOWER SLOPES. **OPPOSITE, TOP:** THE NATAL BOTTLEBRUSH. **OPPOSITE, BOTTOM:** RED HOT POKERS BRIGHTEN THE SUMMER SCENERY.

MOUNTAIN SEASONS

IN SUMMER DRAMATIC THUNDERSTORMS OCCUR ALMOST EVERY AFTERNOON, AND THE HILLS ARE FLUSHED WITH GREEN GRASS AND A RICH VARIETY OF PLANTS AND FLOWERS.

For flower-lovers, this is the best time to be in the Berg. The biological diversity of the mountains is exceptional, with 2,153 plant species, including spectacular shows of orchids and irises, and 299 bird, 48 mammal, 48 reptile and 26 frog species. Approximately 119 of these species of plants and animals are under threat of extinction and are listed in the Red Data Book as endangered.

MOUNTAIN SEASONS

WHEN WINTER COMES AND NIGHT-TIME TEMPERATURES DROP BELOW FREEZING, THE GREEN HILLS TURN A FROST-BITTEN, GOLDEN BROWN. Many of the smaller creatures hibernate in small caves and summer migrants fly north to warmer climates. This is a time of stark contrasts – while the air is crisp, with little chance of afternoon thunderstorms, sudden bad weather and snow means that hikers should always be prepared for the unexpected. In mid- to late winter, park officials and farmers start to burn blocks of dry grass to remove plant material in order to stimulate new growth, which can leave the skies a little hazy.

OPPOSITE, TOP: WINTER HIKERS IN LOTENI IN THE SOUTHERN BERG.

OPPOSITE, BOTTOM: AN AERIAL VIEW OF THE WINTER-BROWN DRAKENSBERG FOOTHILLS. **LEFT:** A MOUNTAIN POOL AT GIANT'S HUT IN THE GIANT'S CASTLE GAME RESERVE.

ABOVE: THE SUMMER GRASSES TURN GOLDEN BROWN IN WINTER.

BELOW: HELICHRYSUMS OR EVERLASTINGS.

OFTEN, AFTER DAYS OF CLOUD AND RAIN, THE WEATHER CLEARS AND THE MOUNTAINS ARE REVEALED COVERED WITH A POWDERING OF WHITE SNOW. SNOWFALLS OCCUR BETWEEN SIX AND 12 TIMES A YEAR, WITH THE HEAVIEST FALLS BEING EXPERIENCED ON THE SUMMIT IN WINTER. Severe storms can, however, occur at any time at these high altitudes, and even in summer hikers should anticipate sudden turns in the weather. The snow is seldom more than about a metre thick, and this decreases sharply with declining altitude. In the lower areas the snow usually melts within a day or two, whereas in the south-facing gulleys of the High Berg it can remain all year round.

OPPOSITE, TOP: THE THUKELA FALLS CREATE A SUPREME CHALLENGE FOR ICE-CLIMBERS IN WINTER. **OPPOSITE, BOTTOM:** SNOW ON THE LOWER SLOPES USUALLY MELTS A FEW DAYS AFTER THE STORM. **ABOVE:** THE SNOW-COVERED PEAKS OF GIANT'S CASTLE. **BELOW LEFT:** MONK'S COWL GULLEY IN ITS WINTER WHITES. **BELOW RIGHT:** A WELL-EQUIPPED HIKER BATTLES UP THE KAMASHILENGA PASS IN LOTENI.

THE LITTLE BERG

EXTENDING EASTWARDS FROM THE MIGHTY MOUNTAINS ARE A SERIES OF GRASS-COVERED RIDGES THAT TERMINATE IN PROMINENT SANDSTONE CLIFFS. THIS IS THE LITTLE BERG – A DELIGHTFUL AREA TO EXPLORE.

Most Drakensberg resorts and campsites are located in this area of gentle hills, valleys and rivers. It is also where the San once made their homes beneath sandstone overhangs.

OPPOSITE, TOP LEFT: ZULU VILLAGES IN THE FOOTHILLS. **OPPOSITE, TOP RIGHT:** ELAND, THE LARGEST OF ALL ANTELOPE, OCCUR IN HERDS IN THE MOUNTAINS. **BELOW LEFT:** A TYPICAL LITTLE BERG SCENE. **RIGHT:** WASH-DAY IN THE BERG. **BELOW RIGHT:** LOCAL RESIDENTS.

The Little Berg lies mostly below 2,000 metres and is less prone to weather extremes, which makes it relatively safe for hiking. It is also in this area that most of the region's animals, plants and insects are found. Likely sightings include eland, baboon, mountain rhebok and dassie. Leopard are known to inhabit the area, and occasionally people are lucky enough to see one slinking into a cave. There is fierce competition for grazing, particularly in winter, and many of the eland, common reedbuck and other species migrate from the Little Berg to lower altitudes to find more palatable fields in which to roam and feed to survive.

11

THE HIGH BERG

LEFT: A HIKER BRACES HERSELF AGAINST THE ICY WINDS ON THE TOP OF THE THUKELA FALLS. **ABOVE:** A BASOTHO HORSEMAN AT SANI TOP. **BELOW:** SLOGGETT'S ICE RAT, AN ENDEMIC SPECIES FOUND ONLY AT THE SUMMIT PLATEAU.

TOWERING PEAKS REACHING OVER 3,400 METRES; CLIFFS AND SLOPES OF MORE THAN 2,000 METRES, INCLUDING SOME OF THE MOST SPECTACULAR SCENERY – THIS IS WHAT AWAITS THE VISITOR TO THE HIGH BERG.

These high regions experience intense solar radiation, high evaporation and low average temperatures, with enormous differences in temperature between day and night. Many species found in the Lower Berg are unable to survive these extreme conditions and are not seen at these altitudes. A few, such as the Sloggett's ice rat and some endemic lizards, are specially adapted to the conditions on the High Berg and do not occur below 2,500 metres. Above 2,700 metres only grasses, dwarf shrubs and low, hardy, cushion-forming succulents are able to survive. Some of these plants have special cells that contain high concentrations of solution that act as an 'anti-freeze'. The summit of the Berg has a few Basotho settlements where herders tend their goats during the summer months, but it is mostly unpopulated and prone to sudden changes in weather.

ABOVE: THE ALPINE VEGETATION FOUND ON THE SUMMIT OF THE BERG IS EXTREMELY HARDY.

BELOW: A BASOTHO MAN AT SEHLABATHEBE NATIONAL PARK IN THE LESOTHO HIGHLANDS.

MOUNTAIN BIRDS

ABOVE LEFT: CAPE ROCK THRUSHES ARE FOUND ON MONTANE SLOPES THROUGHOUT THE BERG. **ABOVE RIGHT:** CAPE VULTURES ROOST IN THE ROCKY RAMPARTS OF THE DRAKENSBERG. **BELOW LEFT:** THE MAJESTIC BLACK EAGLE WHICH SWOOPS LOW OVER THE ROCKY GORGES LOOKING FOR SMALL MAMMALS. **BELOW RIGHT:** THE CLUCKING OF HELMETED GUINEA FOWL IS A COMMON SOUND IN THE REST CAMPS OF THE LITTLE BERG. **OPPOSITE, TOP:** PIED KINGFISHERS WORK IN PAIRS OR SMALL PARTIES NEAR RIVERS AND LAKES. **OPPOSITE, BOTTOM:** LAMMERGEYERS, OR BEARDED VULTURES, DROP BONES FROM HIGH ALTITUDES TO CRACK THEM ON THE ROCKS.

A treat awaits bird-watchers, especially in the summer. The wide skies silhouette the graceful shapes of raptors floating on the updrafts, and the Giant's Castle area is well known for its vulture restaurants, where animal carcasses are provided. Nearly 300 species of birds have been recorded in the Drakensberg. Of these 32 species are endemic. Specials include the lammergeyer, Cape vulture, wattled crane, bald ibis and orange-breasted rock-jumper.

THE DRAKENSBERG RANGE
Devil's Knuckle 3,028m
Hodgson's Peak 3,257m
Thaba Ntlenyana (Highest point in Southern Africa) 3,482m
Giant's Castle 3,314m
Champagne Castle 3,377m
Cathkin Peak 3,181m
Cathedral Peak 3,004m
Eastern Buttress 3,047m
Mont-aux-Sources 3,282m
San Paintings
Free State
R74
LITTLE SWITZERLAND
Oliviershoek Pass
Kilburn Dam
THE CAVERN BERG RESORT
Rugged Glen Nature Reserve
MONT-AUX-SOURCES
WITSIESHOEK
TENDELE
The Sentinel 3,165m
Royal Natal National Park
Thukela Falls
Mont-aux-Sources 3,282m
THE AMPHITHEATRE
Woodstock Dam
Zand
Toll Gate
N3
R103
R602
Ventersspruit
R616
Ladysmith
Spioenkop Dam Nature Reserve
R600
Roosboom
Thukela
Bergville
Spioenkop Dam
Mnweni
Mlambonja
Little Thukela
Winterton
Colenso
DRAKENSBERG
SOUTH AFRICA
Khubedu
Cathedral Peak 3,004m
Cathedral Peak State Forest
CATHEDRAL PEAK
Champagne Valley
Ardmore
Frere
DRAKENSBERG SUN
Monk's Cowl State Forest
Sterk
Drakensberg Boys' Choir
Cathkin Peak 3,181m
MONK'S COWL
CHAMPAGNE CASTLE

uKhahlamba-Drakensberg Park

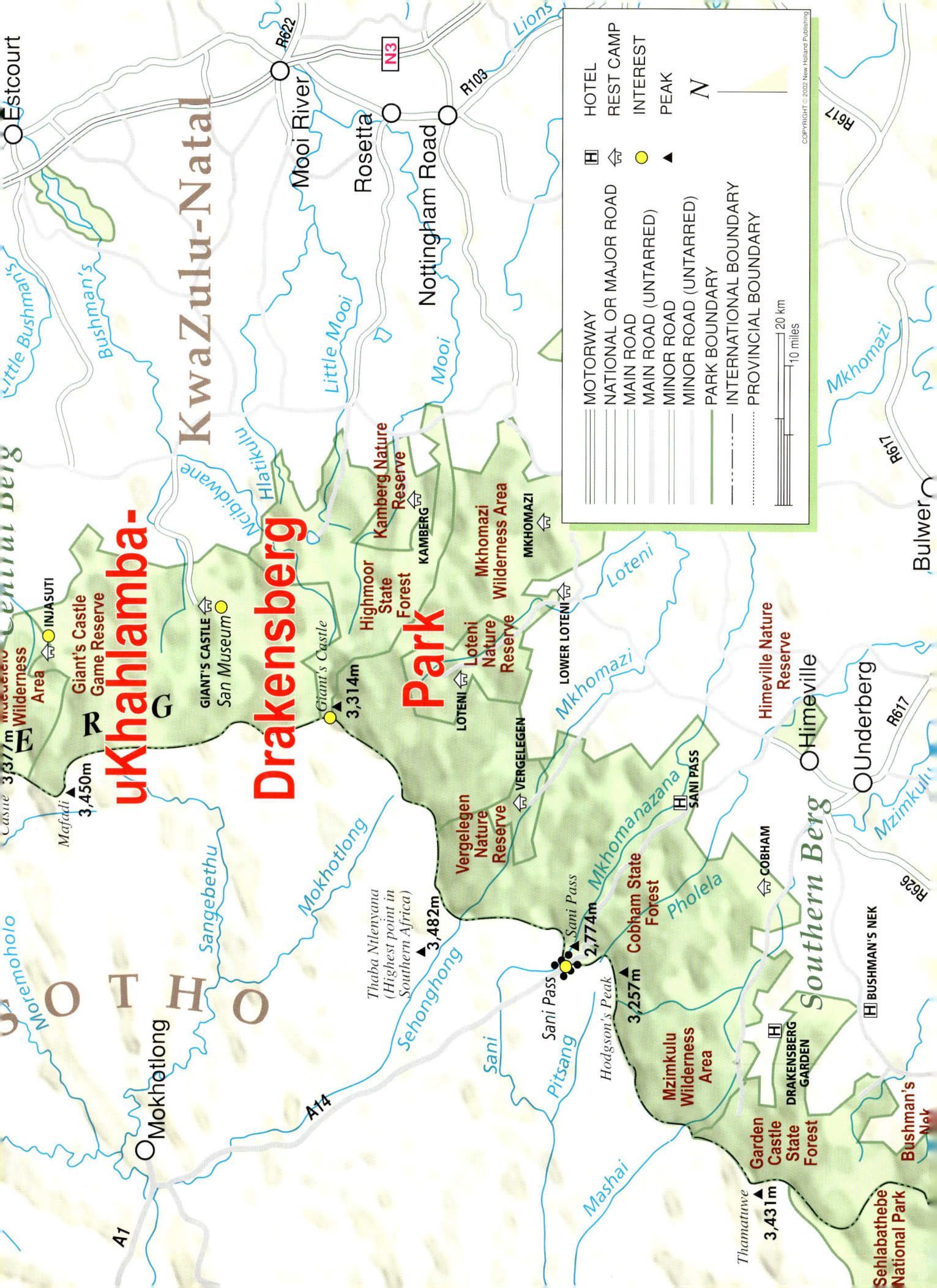

Map Legend
- HOTEL
- REST CAMP
- INTEREST
- PEAK

- MOTORWAY
- NATIONAL OR MAJOR ROAD
- MAIN ROAD
- MAIN ROAD (UNTARRED)
- MINOR ROAD
- MINOR ROAD (UNTARRED)
- PARK BOUNDARY
- INTERNATIONAL BOUNDARY
- PROVINCIAL BOUNDARY

Scale: 20 km / 10 miles

N

COPYRIGHT © 2002 New Holland Publishing

Places and Features

KwaZulu-Natal
- Estcourt
- Mooi River
- Rosetta
- Nottingham Road
- Bulwer
- Himeville
- Underberg

Central Berg
- Injasuti
- Giant's Castle Game Reserve
- Mdedelelo Wilderness Area
- GIANT'S CASTLE San Museum
- Giant's Castle 3,314m
- Mafadi 3,450m
- 3,377m

uKhahlamba-Drakensberg Park
- Kamberg Nature Reserve (KAMBERG)
- Highmoor State Forest
- Mkhomazi Wilderness Area (MKHOMAZI)
- Loteni Nature Reserve (LOTENI)
- LOWER LOTENI
- Vergelegen Nature Reserve (VERGELEGEN)
- Mkhomanazana
- Sani Pass 2,774m
- SANI PASS
- Cobham State Forest (COBHAM)
- Hodgson's Peak 3,257m
- Mzimkulu Wilderness Area
- DRAKENSBERG GARDEN
- Garden Castle State Forest
- Thamatuwe 3,431m

Southern Berg
- Himeville Nature Reserve
- BUSHMAN'S NEK
- Bushman's Nek
- Sehlabathebe National Park

LESOTHO
- Mokhotlong
- Thaba Ntlenyana (Highest point in Southern Africa) 3,482m

Rivers
Little Bushman's, Bushman's, Lions, Mooi, Little Mooi, Ncibidwane, Hlatikulu, Loteni, Mkhomazi, Mzimkulu, Mkhomazi, Sangebethu, Mokhotlong, Moremoholo, Sehonghong, Sani, Pitsang, Pholela, Mashai

Roads
A1, A14, N3, R103, R617, R622, R626

ABOVE: POLYCHROME IMAGES IN A SANDSTONE OVERHANG AT KAMBERG IN THE SOUTHERN BERG.

FROM THE LATE STONE AGE UNTIL THE MID-19TH CENTURY, THE SAN LIVED IN THE SANDSTONE CAVES OF THE LITTLE BERG, HUNTING ELAND AND GATHERING PLANTS. BUT THEIR LIVES WERE DISRUPTED IN THE 1800S BY ENCROACHING SETTLEMENT IN THE REGION.

These days the only clues to their way of life are the colourful rock paintings in the sandstone overhangs. It is estimated that some 35 per cent of all rock art sites in South Africa are in the Berg, and are among the most impressive. There are about 600 sites with more than 40,000 images. Experts have identified similarities between rock art throughout the world and suggest that they were the works of shamans who were in a state of trance, during which they communicated much about their relationship with animals and the spirit world. These artworks are delicate and protected by law, and visitors should take care not to touch them.

ROCK ART HERITAGE

OPPOSITE, BOTTOM: IMAGES OF SAN AT THE BATTLE CAVE NEAR INJASUTI. **ABOVE LEFT:** SAN CHASING ANTELOPE (BATTLE CAVE). **LEFT:** A LEOPARD AT GIANT'S CASTLE. **ABOVE RIGHT:** ELAND SCENES ARE THE MOST COMMON. **BELOW:** A LIFE-SIZED MUSEUM AT GAME PASS SHELTER NEAR GIANT'S CASTLE REST CAMP.

MOUNTAIN EXPLORATION

BELOW: A POPULAR WALK LEADS FROM THE ROYAL NATAL NATIONAL PARK THROUGH THE THUKELA GORGE TO THE BASE OF THE AMPHITHEATRE.

OPPOSITE, TOP LEFT: MOST DAY WALKS ARE ALONG SMOOTHLY CONTOURED PATHS THROUGH THE HILLS OF THE LITTLE BERG.

ABOVE: GOOD STURDY BOOTS, AND PREFERABLY ONES THAT WILL STAY DRY INSIDE, ARE RECOMMENDED FOR THE BERG. **BELOW:** THE PATHS NEAR RESORTS ARE SIGNPOSTED SO YOU CAN FIND YOUR WAY EASILY.

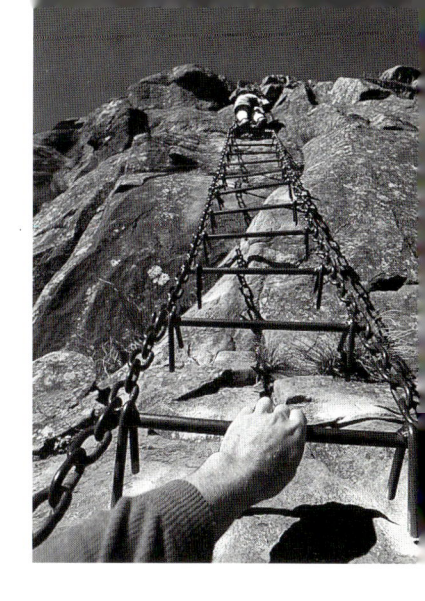

ABOVE: THE EASIEST WALK TO THE SUMMIT PLATEAU IS VIA THE SENTINEL AND TWO SETS OF CHAIN LADDERS. **BELOW:** THERE ARE BASIC MOUNTAIN HUTS FOR HIKERS.

Hikers have been putting on their boots and venturing into the Drakensberg hills since the 1930s. The popular trails are mostly well marked and vary from one-hour rambles to multi-day trips designed for the most experienced of hikers. Most people usually stay in the rolling hills of the Little Berg, where the weather is milder and the greatest diversity of animals and plants can be found. But for the adventurous there are also several paths to the summit where outstanding views can be enjoyed. Anyone heading into the mountains should fill in the mountain register. High winds, icy cold and snow in winter and thunder showers experienced virtually every afternoon in summer present potential dangers to the unwary hiker.

THE BERG'S RARIFIED AIR AND DRAMATIC MOUNTAIN SCENERY HAVE INSPIRED GENERATIONS OF ADVENTURERS. THE FIRST EXPLORERS WERE FRENCH MISSIONARIES IN THE LATE 1700S AND SINCE THEN A SUCCESSION OF MOUNTAIN CLIMBERS HAS COME HERE TO TEST THEIR SKILLS, FIND NEW ROUTES – AND CONQUER THEM.

Among the most famous of these was a bricklayer from New Zealand named George Thomson who was the first to climb many of the peaks, particularly in the Cathedral Peak area. Today outdoor enthusiasts test their mettle on horseback, mountain bikes and paragliders. The Sani Pass is a most exciting 4x4 drive to Lesotho, along a switchback route originally used by Basotho horsemen to reach the top of the Berg.

TOP: CATHEDRAL PEAK HOTEL OFFERS TOURISTS PICNICS IN THE HIGH BERG – TRANSPORT PROVIDED BY HELICOPTER. **LEFT:** THE GENTLE HILLS MAKE THE LITTLE BERG WONDERFUL HORSE-RIDING COUNTRY.

ABOVE: A MOUNTAIN BIKER ON THE SUMMIT OF THE BERG.

RIGHT: A VEHICLE NEGOTIATES THE SWITCHBACKS OF THE SANI PASS. **BELOW:** MANY RESORTS OFFER ACTIVITIES AND WALKS THAT ARE SUITABLE FOR CHILDREN.

23

MOUNTAIN WATERS

On a hike there is nothing quite as refreshing as taking a sip of clear water directly from a mountain stream – or plunging into an icy pool. The water in the Drakensberg is filtered through rock and grass and enters the streams perfectly clean and sediment free. Water conservation is one of the best reasons for protecting these mountains: the Drakensberg watershed feeds the three largest rivers in KwaZulu-Natal – the Thukela, the Mkhomazi and the Mzimkulu. Their protection is of enormous economic importance to the country. Owing to the steep gradients and the shallow soil, most of the rainfall (about 600 mm a year) leaves the Berg as run-off. The only way to maintain this situation is to keep the indigenous vegetation in a pristine state and limit alien plantations and development.

OPPOSITE, TOP: MOUNTAIN POOLS ARE ALIVE WITH INSECTS, FISH AND PLANTS. **OPPOSITE, BOTTOM LEFT:** WATERFALLS AND POOLS OFFER WONDERFUL SWIMMING, BUT HIKERS ARE URGED NOT TO POLLUTE THEM WITH CHEMICALS SUCH AS SOAP AND SUNTAN CREAM. **OPPOSITE, BOTTOM RIGHT:** AN IDEAL SPOT FOR REST AND REFLECTION. **ABOVE:** A HIKER RELAXES AT A FAST-FLOWING STREAM NEAR GIANT'S CASTLE. **BELOW:** THE CASCADES IN THE ROYAL NATAL NATIONAL PARK.

BELOW: WAITING FOR A RISE AT LAKE NAVERONE.

OPPOSITE, TOP: FISHING REGULATIONS DICTATE THAT NO LIVE BAIT – ONLY FLIES – MAY BE USED TO CATCH TROUT IN THE DRAKENSBERG.

ABOVE: A TROUT FISHERMAN CASTS HIS LINE INTO A STILL LAKE NEAR KAMBERG.

BELOW: A LARGE BROWN TROUT FROM KAMBERG HATCHERY.

2 6

FLY FISHING

For the early settlers in the Drakensberg there was just one thing missing from the region – trout! In 1890 the first brown trout were imported from England and a few years later rainbow trout were brought in from America.

These fish are now found in all streams and rivers in the Drakensberg, with rainbow being common in the Pholela, Mzimkulu and Mzimvubu rivers, and brown trout dominating the Bushman's, Mooi and Loteni rivers. Every year more than 6,000 anglers come to test their skills in these waters. The river fishing season is usually limited to September to June, while dams are open throughout the year. The Drakensberg minnow is an endemic fish, first identfied in 1938. It was thought to be extinct, but a small population was rediscovered in 1970 in a river in Sehlabathebe.

ACCOMMODATION

KWAZULU-NATAL WILDLIFE OFFERS A RANGE OF PLACES TO REST YOUR HEAD, MOST OF WHICH ARE EXCELLENT VALUE FOR MONEY IN SOME OF THE MOST PRISTINE PARTS OF THE BERG.

These include self-catering chalets at Giant's Castle, Injasuti and Loteni campsites, as well as mountain huts and caves for camping. Furthermore there are dozens of excellent family hotels offering full board and a host of activities from horse-riding to bowls and guided walks.

OPPOSITE, TOP: THE SELF-CATERING HUTS AT TENDELE ARE SITUATED AT THE BASE OF THE AMPHITHEATRE IN THE ROYAL NATAL NATIONAL PARK. **OPPOSITE, BOTTOM LEFT:** THE CATHEDRAL PEAK HOTEL OFFERS FULL BOARD AND HOTEL ACTIVITIES. **OPPOSITE, BOTTOM RIGHT:** MANY DRAKENSBERG HOTELS ARE FAMILY ORIENTATED WITH FACILITIES FOR ACTIVITIES SUCH AS TENNIS AND BOWLS. **ABOVE:** THE INJASUTI REST CAMP IS IN AN ISOLATED VALLEY BENEATH SOME OF THE HIGHEST PEAKS IN THE BERG. **RIGHT:** MONT-AUX-SOURCES IS AN EXCELLENT PRIVATE HOTEL BENEATH THE AMPHITHEATRE.

MOUNTAIN CRAFTS

ABOVE: ARTISTS DECORATING POTTERY AT ARDMORE STUDIO IN CHAMPAGNE VALLEY. **ABOVE RIGHT:** COMPLETED POTTERY ON DISPLAY, READY FOR SALE. **BELOW:** A WEAVING STUDIO OFFERS EMPLOYMENT IN THE CENTRAL DRAKENSBERG, PRODUCING FINE EXAMPLES OF LOCAL ARTS AND CRAFTWARE. **OPPOSITE, TOP:** MOST OF THE CRAFTS – SUCH AS THESE WALKING STICKS – ARE MADE FROM ALIEN VEGETATION. **RIGHT:** SPLENDID EXAMPLES OF ZULU-WOVEN BASKETS AT A ROADSIDE STALL NEAR CATHEDRAL PEAK.

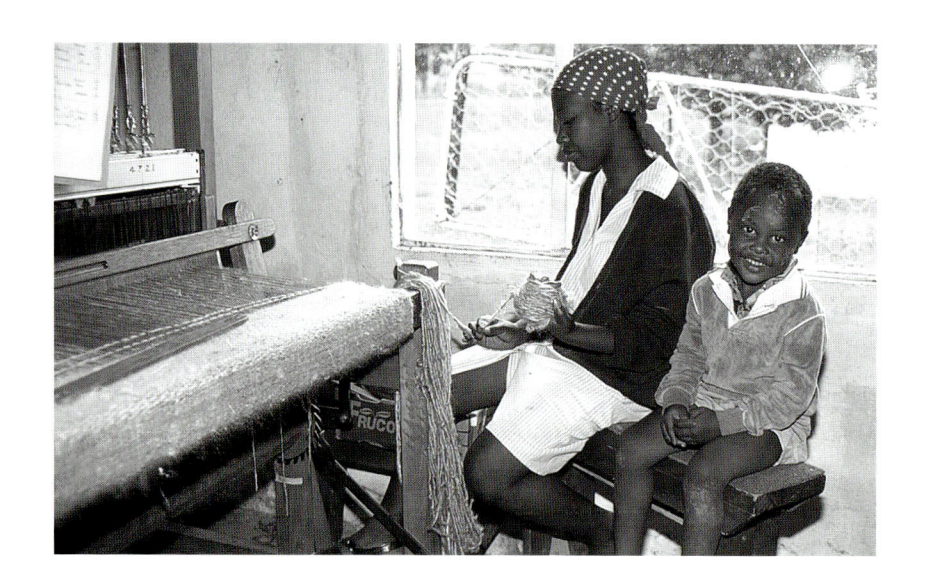

The wide skies, towering peaks and clean air of the Drakensberg inspire many artistic people living in the foothills of the mountains. One of the best-known art galleries is Ardmore Studio, a collective of some 40 Zulu and Sotho artists whose works are sold and marketed worldwide. Many other artists in the southern and central areas have also opened their galleries and studios to the public and excellent craft routes have been established. Also inspired by these mountains are the students of the Drakensberg Boys' Choir. The sounds of their music have been filtering out of the Monk's Cowl region of Champagne Valley for about half a century, and the boys have performed to appreciative audiences across the world.

ABOVE: WASHING DAY IN THE DRAKENSBERG FOOTHILLS.

OPPOSITE: ROCK ART IN THE KAMBERG.

FRONT COVER, CLOCKWISE FROM TOP LEFT: BLACK EAGLE; GIANT'S CASTLE; RED HOT POKERS; ROYAL NATAL NATIONAL PARK; BERG HORSE-RIDERS; CHAIN LADDERS, THE SENTINEL; SAN PAINTING AT BATTLE CAVE; THE CASCADES; **BACK COVER, CLOCKWISE FROM TOP LEFT:** KAMASHILENGA PASS IN LOTENI; SEHLABATHEBE NATIONAL PARK; NEAR COBHAM, LITTLE BERG; MEMBERS OF THE DRAKENSBERG BOYS' CHOIR; TROUT FISHING ON LAKE NAVERONE; CAMPERS, LOTENI; BERG ATTRACTIONS; LOCAL HANDIWORK.

First published in 2002 by Struik Publishers
(a division of New Holland Publishing (South Africa) (Pty) Ltd)
London • Cape Town • Sydney • Auckland

Garfield House
86–88 Edgware Road
W2 2EA London
United Kingdom
www.newhollandpublishers.com

80 McKenzie Street
Cape Town
8001
South Africa
www.struik.co.za

14 Aquatic Drive
Frenchs Forest
NSW 2086
Australia

218 Lake Road
Northcote,
Auckland
New Zealand

New Holland Publishing is a member of the Johnnic Publishing Group

10 9 8 7 6 5 4 3 2 1

ISBN 1 86872 740 8

Copyright © 2002 in published edition: Struik Publishers
Copyright © 2002 in photographs: as credited below
Copyright © 2002 in text: David Rogers
Copyright © 2002 in map on page 16–17: Struik Publishers

Publishing manager: Annlerie van Rooyen
Managing editor: Lesley Hay-Whitton
Design director: Janice Evans
Concept design: Michelle Ludek
Designer: Alison Day
Editors: Helen Keevy and Yazeed Fakier
Picture researcher: Carmen Watts
Cartographer: John Loubser

Reproduction by Hirt & Carter Cape (Pty) Ltd
Printed by Craft Print Pte Ltd

All rights reserved. No part of this publication may be reproduced, stored in a retrieval system or transmitted, in any form or by any means, electronic, mechanical, photocopying or otherwise, without the prior written permission of the publishers and copyright holders.

PHOTOGRAPHIC CREDITS
Copyright for the photographs rests with David Rogers, with the exception of those listed below where it rests with the following photographers and/or with their agents: SA=Shaen Adey; KB=Karl Beath; DDP= Dennis/De la Harpe Photography; RDLH=Roger de la Harpe; NJD=Nigel J Dennis; WD=Wendy Dennis; WK=Walter Knirr; PA= Photo Access; SIL=Struik Image Library; AW=Alan Wilson.
FRONT COVER: (pics numbered clockwise from top left) **1.** NJD/SIL, **3.** RDLH/DDP, **4.** SA/SIL, **5.** WK, **7.** SA/SIL, **8.** SA/SIL;
BACK COVER: (pics numbered clockwise from top left) **1.** KB, **4.** RDLH/DDP, **5.** SA/SIL, **6.** KB, **8.** SA/SIL; **INSIDE FRONT COVER**: RDLH/SIL; **p. 1**: SA/SIL; **p. 2/3**: (centre) SA/SIL; **p. 3**: (bottom) WK/SIL; **p. 4**: (top) WK/SIL; **p. 4/5**: (centre) SA/SIL; **p. 5**: (bottom right) RDLH/DDP; **p. 6**: (top) KB; **p. 8**: (top) KB, (bottom) NJD/DDP; **p. 9**: (top) NJD/DDP, (bottom left & right) KB; **p. 12**: (bottom) RDLH/DDP; **p. 14**: (top & bottom right) NJD /SIL, (bottom left) RDLH/SIL; **p. 14/15**: (centre) RDLH/DDP; **p. 15**: (top) NJD/DDP, (bottom) RDLH/SIL; **p. 18**: (top left): SA/SIL; **p. 19**: (top right) SA/SIL, (bottom) RDLH/SIL; **p. 23**: (top left) KB, (bottom) SA/SIL; **p. 25**: (bottom) SA/SIL; **p. 26**: top SA/SIL; **p. 26/27**: (centre) WD/SIL; **p. 28**: (top) SA/SIL, (bottom left) AW/PA; **p. 29**: (top) SA/SIL; **p. 30**: (top left & right) RDLH/DDP; **p. 31**: (top) SA/SIL, (bottom) WK/SIL; **INSIDE BACK COVER**: SA/SIL.